HANDLING FAMILY CHALLENGES

By Rebecca Rowell

CONTENT CONSULTANT

Dr. Amy Bellmore
Professor of Human Development
University of Wisconsin–Madison

Essential Library

An Imprint of Abdo Publishing | abdobooks.com

abdobooks.com

Published by Abdo Publishing, a division of ABDO, PO Box 398166, Minneapolis, Minnesota 55439. Copyright © 2021 by Abdo Consulting Group, Inc. International copyrights reserved in all countries. No part of this book may be reproduced in any form without written permission from the publisher. Essential Library™ is a trademark and logo of Abdo Publishing.

Printed in the United States of America, North Mankato, Minnesota.
082020
012021

Cover Photo: LightField Studios/Shutterstock Images
Interior Photos: iStockphoto, 8, 12, 15, 20, 22, 27, 34, 42, 48, 57, 59, 61, 80, 84, 92, 95, 96, 98; Art Well/Shutterstock Images, 10; Sol Stock/iStockphoto, 16; LightField Studios/Shutterstock Images, 28; Jaren Wicklund/iStockphoto, 32, 90; Shutterstock Images, 37, 44, 46, 51, 54, 66, 78; Antonio Guillem/Shutterstock Images, 68; G-Stock Studio/iStockphoto, 71; SDI Productions/iStockphoto, 74; Karen Coxhead/iStockphoto, 82; Juan Monino/iStockphoto, 86

Editor: Aubrey Zalewski
Series Designer: Nikki Nordby

Library of Congress Control Number: 2019954533
Publisher's Cataloging-in-Publication Data

Names: Rowell, Rebecca, author.
Title: Handling family challenges / by Rebecca Rowell
Description: Minneapolis, Minnesota : Abdo Publishing, 2021 | Series: Strong, healthy girls | Includes online resources and index.
Identifiers: ISBN 9781532192180 (lib. bdg.) | ISBN 9781098210083 (ebook)
Subjects: LCSH: Families--Social aspects--Juvenile literature. | Family relationships--Juvenile literature. | Family life--Juvenile literature. | Communication in families--Juvenile literature. | Teenagers--Family relationships--Juvenile literature.
Classification: DDC 155.533--dc23

CONTENTS

DR. AMY

Dr. Amy Bellmore is fascinated by humans and inspired by teens. She works as a professor of human development in the Department of Educational Psychology at the University of Wisconsin–Madison, where she conducts research on the peer relationships of adolescents and teaches courses on adolescent development.

She earned a PhD in developmental psychology at the University of Connecticut. Though she did not declare a major in psychology until the middle of her sophomore year in college, she has evidence that she was destined to study teens from a work aptitude test she took her sophomore year in high school. Based on the results of the test about her interests and skills, she discovered that the best job for her was a research psychologist. Now that she has worked in that career for almost 20 years, she is happy to verify that the test was correct.

During her career, Dr. Amy has conducted numerous studies on the social experiences of teens, which have been published in more than 60 articles and book chapters. Most of these studies take place through partnerships with public middle schools and high schools across Wisconsin that share the goal of promoting the welfare of adolescents. Following the leads of the teens themselves, who have moved parts of their lives to online spaces, Dr. Amy's most recent research attends to the ways teens use social media to create and maintain their social relationships. Dr. Amy loves using social media herself, and she finds this research area particularly exciting because teens create and transform technology in new and different ways. Dr. Amy also serves as an associate editor for the *Journal of Research on Adolescence*, which is the flagship journal for the Society of Research on Adolescence, a community of researchers dedicated to the well-being of adolescents.

In her nonwork life, Dr. Amy stays on the pulse of youth culture (and generally enjoys rocking out) by regularly attending concerts of pop-culture icons. Dr. Amy splits her time between Madison, Wisconsin, and Los Angeles, California, with her adolescent puggles, Presley and Riddock.

TAKE IT

FROM ME

Family. There's no one kind. Families come in all shapes and sizes: one parent, two parents, biological parents, stepparents, foster parents, and more. My family has divorced parents and four kids. Regardless of the makeup, the importance of family is undeniable. Ideally, parents provide food, shelter, and support and teach us about the world. We learn how to socialize through experiences with our family. We see how our parents act in the face of challenges and stress and learn from them—what to do and what not to do.

While families vary, they face many similar challenges. Some situations can be tougher than others. But all of them provide learning opportunities. We learn about our family members, we learn about ourselves, and we learn how to communicate—or how not to. Some family experiences can be incredibly stressful, such as when a parent has a drinking problem. Some aren't as dramatic—or traumatic—but they cause stress for a time, such as when an older sibling moves away.

What's your family like? What do you find special about it? What do you find frustrating? Some of us have great relationships with our family. Some of us don't. Either way, our family experiences leave their mark. I know my family affected me long after I left home. Honestly, I continue to struggle sometimes with members of my family. But good or bad, your family is your family, and it will provide you with a wealth of learning opportunities. Some of them may be like those described in this book. I hope the scenarios you read help you navigate some of the many circumstances that may arise in your family.

Dealing with conflict, issues, and change takes practice. Really, it's a lifelong process. If you don't handle a situation as well as you had hoped, don't fret. Keep moving forward. Another opportunity for you to practice will likely arise. Why? Because that's what happens with families. Be patient. Be strong. Be you.

XOXO,
BECCA

FIRST JOB

Have you had your first job yet? Do you think about getting a job? Getting your first job is a milestone. And like any milestone in your life, it has the ability to be influenced by or affect your family.

I babysat when I was 12 and 13. But my first "real" job was the summer after my sophomore year in high school. I was a dishwasher at a pizza restaurant. I don't remember why I wanted the job, but I do recall that I quit before school started. I also don't remember my parents caring about my having a job. My mom didn't live with us, and my dad was pretty hands off in terms of parenting.

But not all parents and guardians are like that. Maybe your parents encourage you to get a job. Or maybe they don't want you working. Either way, what your parents or guardians want may not line up with what you want. And that disconnect is ripe for conflict. That's what Aisha discovered. She wanted a job and

found a great one at a place she really liked. Plus, it came with perks. What could be better? Getting the job was a cinch—that is, until her grandfather said she couldn't take it.

AISHA'S STORY

Aisha walked down her street. She had walked the route more times than she could remember, but today was different. She was so happy she almost bounced. She was on her way home from school with a detour at Corner Coffee, the local coffee shop and her favorite hangout. Sometimes Aisha met her friends there. Other times, she'd sit there and do her homework. Always, she enjoyed getting something to eat or drink. Today, she stopped by because of something she'd seen in the window: a help wanted sign.

Aisha had recently turned 16 and had decided she wanted to get a job. She loved being around people, and she could save the money for college. She had been keeping her eye out for the perfect job—and working at Corner Coffee was exactly that. Aisha couldn't wait to get home and share the news with her grandparents. They were always so loving and supportive—until, it seemed, Aisha shared her decision over dinner.

Aisha had recently turned 16 and had decided she wanted to get a job.

"How was school today, Aisha?" her grandfather asked.

"It was good," she said. "I got a B on my geometry test. And I met with the homecoming committee to talk about events for homecoming week."

"It sounds like you had a productive day," Grandpa said.

"I did," Aisha said. "I also stopped by Corner Coffee and talked with the owner about working there. I saw a sign in her window that she's hiring. I really like that coffee shop. The muffins are great, and the hot chocolate is so good."

"Work?" Grandpa asked, surprised and kind of firm. "You don't need to work. Don't bother with it."

"What do you mean?" Aisha asked.

"I mean you're not getting a job," he replied.

"But—" Aisha started to say before her grandpa cut her off.

"No *but*, Aisha," he said firmly. "End of discussion."

Aisha looked at her grandpa and then her grandma. She wasn't sure what to say. Her grandpa never talked to her like that. She got up from the table.

"I have a lot of reading to do tonight," Aisha said, holding back her disappointment. "I should probably get started. Thanks for dinner, Gigi."

"But we haven't had dessert," her grandmother replied. "I made peach cobbler. I know how you love my peach cobbler."

TALK ABOUT IT

▪ Have you ever had a family member respond negatively to something you were excited about? What did you do?

▪ What do you think Aisha was feeling?

▪ How would you have reacted if you were Aisha?

Aisha didn't respond, already walking into the kitchen with her dishes.

***

Aisha went to her room and started on her English assignment. She was in the middle of reading a short story when her grandma knocked on her door.

"I thought you might be upset," Gigi said, coming in and sitting on the edge of Aisha's bed. She handed Aisha some cobbler and a spoon. "You know, your grandfather is reasonable."

"I know," Aisha said. "But he didn't even let me tell him about the job. That's not like him."

"I think it may be because of his experience with his first job," Gigi explained. "He was 15 and *had* to work. His family struggled financially, so any income was important. Your grandfather had to give up playing high school sports so he could work

13

Aisha understood that her grandpa's experiences must have been difficult for him.

after school. And he left school after his junior year to take a full-time job."

"Really? I didn't know that. Maybe he thinks I'll end up not finishing school," Aisha said, thinking out loud. "Or that I think he's not doing a good enough job providing for me." She paused. Aisha understood that her grandpa's experiences must have been difficult for him. But that didn't change what she wanted, and she knew that there was no chance she'd quit school for her job at Corner Coffee. Her grandpa didn't have to worry.

"I should talk to him . . . tonight," Aisha continued. "I still really want that job, and I want him to hear my plan."

"That sounds like a good idea, Aisha," Gigi said.

"Thanks for telling me about Gramps," Aisha said. "And thank

TALK ABOUT IT

= Do you think it was good that Gigi told Aisha about Grandpa's experience? Why or why not?

= Why do you think Gigi shared that story with Aisha?

you for dessert," she added, putting a spoonful in her mouth. "It's delicious."

***

After eating her dessert and finishing her short story, Aisha headed downstairs. Her grandpa was watching a baseball game on TV.

"Gramps?" she asked. "Can I talk to you? I want to tell you about my visit to Corner Coffee today."

"I told you already, you don't need a job," he said.

"I know," she responded, not backing down. "You and Gigi do a great job of providing for me. I'm so glad and so lucky to have you. The thing is, I *want* a job."

"What about school?" he asked.

"I love school," Aisha said enthusiastically. "And work isn't going to interfere with it or my other activities."

Aisha sat down by her grandpa.

"Gigi told me that you had to work when you were my age— even younger than me," Aisha said. "I'm sorry you missed out on things you loved because of it. I'm sorry you didn't graduate." She paused. "That's not going to happen to me, Gramps, because I have you."

"Well," Grandpa replied, his eyes still fixed on the TV, "I certainly hope that doesn't happen. That's not my plan."

"Can I tell you about the job?" Aisha asked. "I'm really excited about it—well, you know, if I take it. I even have a list of reasons why taking the job is a good decision."

Aisha's grandfather turned off the TV and set down the remote.

"OK," he replied, "let's talk about it."

TALK ABOUT IT

- How did knowing her grandpa's story help Aisha?

- Have you ever had to make a parent, grandparent, or other family member listen to you? What was the experience like? Did you get that person to listen? If yes, how?

- What advice would you give a friend who wants to talk to a family member about an important decision?

ASK THE

EXPERT

Feeling disappointed when you don't get the response you want is normal. It's how you respond in the face of no that can make a big difference. When Aisha was upset by her grandfather's response, she stepped away instead of arguing. She kept the disagreement from escalating. She also listened to Gigi's story about Grandpa and tried to understand his point of view.

When a disagreement happens—big or small—you can follow a few steps to get communication going again. First, remove yourself from the situation and take time to regain calm and collect your thoughts. For Aisha, that meant going to her room and focusing on homework. That might work for you too. You could also try taking a walk, listening to music, or even taking a nap.

Next, if appropriate, apologize. Then do your best to understand the other person's reasoning. Ask why he or she said no. Listen, and don't interrupt. Once that person has finished, share your point of view. Do it calmly. If you feel tensions rising, go back to step one and excuse yourself.

Once you both have shared your viewpoints, try to find middle ground. Remember that your parent or guardian wants what's best for you. And keep in mind that guardians make the final decision. Sometimes you simply don't have a say in the matter. Once a decision is made, let it go and move on.

GET **HEALTHY**

- Before asking for something big, consider making a list of talking points for the discussion.

- Be prepared for a negative answer. Think about how you'll respond if you don't get the reply you want.

- Even if you get frustrated, be respectful. Speak calmly, and listen carefully.

- Remember that your family members have histories that have shaped who they are and how they behave—just as the experiences you have now will shape you as an adult.

THE LAST WORD FROM **BECCA**

Growing up, I was afraid to ask for even small things. I didn't want to be told no and feel rejected. Instead of asking my parents directly, I'd leave a note on one of their dressers. My family isn't good at communicating, but I've gotten better at it.

You'll have plenty of chances throughout your life to ask for things you want. It's unlikely that you'll get a yes every time. Sometimes you'll get a no—and it could be of the immediate, firm, no-questions-asked variety. Whether you think you'll be met with a yes or a no, I encourage you to speak up for yourself and what you want. Communicate, and keep communicating. You may just get what you want. Even better, you could have important breakthroughs in understanding each other.

CHAPTER TWO

REMARRIED

Families have their own distinct cultures. Just as countries and ethnic groups have shared traditions, languages, foods, and more, so do families. Family cultures are composed of values, rules—both spoken and unspoken—and traditions. Family norms guide family members, influencing how they dress, talk, and act. A family's culture shapes the children growing up in it. The culture can have both good and bad elements. For example, I learned to avoid conflict growing up. I remember seeing my parents start to argue and my mom simply walk away. That image stuck. For a long time, I clammed up in the face of conflict. That's what I knew. That was my family's culture. But we had good elements too. On many Sundays, my dad made breakfast for us. He'd make pancakes or French toast for us kids and an omelet for Mom.

Norms, traditions, and routines unite a family. But life changes, such as the addition or loss of a family member, can drastically alter a family's culture. Sandra and her mom had their life together. They were a team, and Sandra knew she could always rely on her mom to be there for things big and small. But then her mom got engaged. Amid the fun of preparing for the wedding, Sandra realized that life as she knew it was going to change dramatically. And the thought of that change was overwhelming.

SANDRA'S STORY

Sandra was an only child. She and her mom had been on their own for a long time. Sandra was 16, and her parents had divorced when she was five. She saw her dad every other weekend and every other holiday. Sandra spent most of her time with her mom, and the two were very close. They took adventures to the zoo,

and they went to movies, fairs, and museums together. Last year, they visited at least one bakery a month to find the best doughnuts in the city. One of her favorite traditions with her mom was the simplest. Every Thursday they would nestle into the couch with pillows, blankets, and snacks to watch a movie. Those nights were perfect. Sandra knew she could count on her mom for anything.

Sandra spent most of her time with her mom, and the two were very close.

Sometimes Greg, her mom's boyfriend, would join Sandra and her mom on their outings. Mom had met Greg a little over a year ago. A mutual friend had introduced them. Mom had gone on a few dates before she started seeing Greg, but nothing had ever developed into a relationship. This time was different. Mom and Greg hit it off big-time.

Sandra liked Greg. He was nice, and he made her laugh. Greg seemed to be truly interested in Sandra. He asked her about school and her dance class. He took Sandra and her mom out for dinner, and he sometimes showed up with a pizza or Chinese food. He'd even get an extra fortune cookie or two because he knew how much Sandra liked them. Most of the time, though, Sandra had her mom all to herself.

***

One Sunday, Greg was over for dinner. That wasn't new. He liked to cook, and he and Sandra's mom had fun in the kitchen. Greg made her mom smile and laugh, and Sandra liked that.

TALK ABOUT IT

- Do you have special activities you do regularly with your family? What are they?
- What effects can activities and traditions have on a family?
- What makes a good tradition?

When the two realized they were out of an important ingredient they needed, Sandra's mom ran to the store. That's when Greg shared a secret. He pulled a small, felt-covered box out of his pocket and slid it across the counter toward Sandra. When Sandra opened it, a ring glittered inside. It had a large diamond in the middle, with small diamonds circling it.

"It's just like from a movie," Sandra said.

"I want to ask your mom to marry me," Greg said. "Is that OK, Sandra? May I have your permission?"

"My permission?" Sandra said. "Really?"

"Yes," he replied. "Marrying your mom will make us a family. I want you to be OK with it."

Sandra paused. So many thoughts ran through her head. Greg would become her stepdad, but she already had a dad.

And if her mom married Greg, he'd be at their house more often. He'd *live* with them. What would that mean for her relationship with her mom? Would they still have movie nights? Would they go hunting for the city's best doughnuts? But Sandra couldn't say any of that to Greg. She had to say something nice.

TALK ABOUT IT

= Why do you think Greg wanted Sandra's permission to marry her mom?

= How could Greg's joining their family change the family culture?

= Have you had to deal with divorced parents or dating parents? What was that like? If you haven't, what might it be like?

"Sandra?" Greg said. "Do you approve?"

"Yes, of course," Sandra said, pausing. "The ring is so pretty, Greg. I think Mom will love it."

***

During dinner, Greg proposed to Sandra's mom. She cried tears of joy and said yes immediately. The couple began talking about the future. Over the next several months, the wedding plans began to take shape. Sandra liked watching her mom try on wedding gowns, and she enjoyed trying on dresses herself, looking for just the right one for the special day. Sandra got to see lots of pretty flowers. And she really liked the many slices of different cakes Mom brought home from the cake tasting. Planning the wedding was fun, and Sandra was happy to help her mom. Still, finalizing each decision made the change ahead that much more real.

One evening, Greg showed up with dinner. Mom opened the door when the doorbell rang. "Well, hello, Mr. Clark," she said, giving him a kiss.

"And hello to you, Mrs. Clark-to-be," he said. Mom laughed.

That's when the reality of the situation really hit Sandra. *Mrs. Clark*, she thought. Sandra started to panic. With all the fun and excitement of planning the wedding, she had been distracted from thinking much more about the big changes that Mom and Greg's marriage would cause. But as Greg headed into the kitchen to set the table for dinner, the thoughts she'd had the night of the proposal flooded back.

Mom turned toward the living room. "Time for pizza, Sandra," she said.

Sandra didn't move. She just stared, overwhelmed. Her mom continued calling for her, but Sandra didn't respond. She sniffled. Her mom came into the living room.

> That's when the reality of the situation really hit Sandra. Mrs. Clark, she thought. Sandra started to panic.

"Sandra, what's wrong?" she asked.

Sandra blinked, and tears ran down her cheeks.

"Talk to me," Mom said. "What's going on?"

"Mrs. Clark," Sandra said. "You're going to be Mrs. Clark. We won't have the same last name anymore." She looked at her mom, then closed her eyes. More tears streamed down her cheeks. Mom wrapped her arms around her. Sandra continued. "Things are never going to be the same. Greg will always be here now. I mean, you know, once we're all living together."

"It's going to be an adjustment, that's for sure," Mom said. "And some things may just take time and practice. We're going to have to work things out as a family."

"A family?" Sandra asked.

"Of course," said Mom. "We're going to be a family. Instead of having only a mom and a dad, you'll also have a stepdad." Mom paused, then asked, "You know what that means?"

Mom looked beyond Sandra. Greg was standing nearby. He had heard the conversation. Greg walked to a nearby chair and sat down.

"It means you now have another person on your side who loves you and cares for you and is going to look out for you," Greg explained.

Sandra knew that Greg cared about her. He had already shown her that. But she still worried that she would lose time with her mom. When she said this to Greg, he told Sandra that he wasn't there to get between her and her mom.

TALK ABOUT IT

- Why do you think Sandra responded the way she did?

- If you were in Sandra's shoes, how do you think you would feel?

- What do you think it would be like to have a parent remarry? What are some challenges you might face? How could you overcome them?

"Of course you two will keep doing things together without me," he said. "And sometimes, just you and I can do things together. I'm here for your mom and for you, Sandra."

Mom reassured Sandra. "Our family life is changing—there's no way around that—but it's a good thing. It'll just take some getting used to. I think great things are ahead."

"I get it," Sandra replied. She thought that including Greg in a movie night once in a while could be fun. Maybe they could come up with new traditions that included all three of them.

When she suggested this to her mom, Mom said, "It sounds like a good topic to talk about over dinner. Would you like to have some pizza now? Greg got your favorite."

"Yes, please," Sandra said.

"Great," Mom replied. "Let's eat!"

ASK THE

EXPERT

Sandra's experience of having a parent remarry is common. When a parent remarries, family dynamics change. They have to because a new person—more than one if stepsiblings are involved—is now part of the family. Understand that you aren't losing your parent and that the stepparent isn't replacing your other parent.

As the family adjusts to these changes, bumps are to be expected. One example is in the space itself. Another person will be in the house. You may need to figure out bathroom time. And the stepparent's belongings will be incorporated into the house too, which will create a new look. Another example is with parenting. Your stepparent may approach parenting differently than your biological parent. If stepsiblings are a part of the picture, you may not get along with them, or they may have habits that you aren't used to. As conflicts inevitably arise, sharing thoughts and feelings and working together will help the transition go as smoothly as possible.

Remember that a new family structure also means that there are new opportunities ahead. The new family will create routines, establish traditions, and develop a culture that's unique.

GET **HEALTHY**

- Share what you're feeling, especially any worries and anxiety. If you don't, your parent can't help you cope with the change or calm any fears.

- Ask your parent and stepparent to include you in family decisions. That way you won't feel like things are simply happening to you.

- If you and your parent have a tradition, make a point of continuing it even after your parent gets remarried. Put it on the calendar where everyone can see it.

- Brainstorm ideas for what you, your parent, and your soon-to-be stepparent can do together.

THE LAST WORD FROM **BECCA**

My parents divorced when I was in high school. Both of them moved on to other relationships. My dad's relationships affected me more because I lived with him. Eventually, he ended up in a long-term relationship. When I was away at college, his girlfriend moved in. She changed the decor in the house I grew up in, and she cooked differently than my parents. Visiting Dad has never been the same, and dealing with the changes was an adjustment.

We have our family culture and know our family to be a certain way. As a result, any change to that culture can be challenging. Adjusting to change can take time, especially when adjusting to big changes like gaining a stepparent. A trick to adjusting is communication. Be open and honest. Give your parent or another person an opportunity to support you and help you cope with the new situation.

CHAPTER THREE

HELPING MOM

I deally, a family helps its members feel safe and secure. Parents shield their children from stress. Sometimes, though, that isn't possible. Circumstances surrounding a parent may unavoidably cause stress to the rest of the family. For example, the parent may become seriously ill or lose a job. In the case of Ebony's family, Ebony's mom had more obligations at work, which left her less time at home. During trying times, other family members can pick up responsibilities to help the family get through the situation. But shouldering these additional responsibilities can cause feelings of anxiety. On top of that, the unpredictability of some situations and the uncertainty of how long they may last only exacerbate those feelings. Families must find ways to cope—both as individual members and as a unit.

EBONY'S STORY

Sixteen-year-old Ebony was close to her mom and her 13-year-old brother, Eric. Their bond had grown even more since her dad had passed away in a car accident a few years earlier. The family of three had fun in the kitchen. Mom was a great cook and had been teaching Ebony how to make some of her favorite dishes. Mom would teach, Ebony would make, and Eric would taste. Tuesday was taco night. And one night each week, they'd have breakfast food for dinner. Wednesday was movie night, and they'd squeeze onto the couch—the dog too—to watch a movie together.

One Wednesday evening, Mom stopped Ebony and Eric as they cleaned up after dinner. "Guys, come here for a minute," she said, heading back to the couch. "I want to talk to you."

Ebony and Eric looked at each other and then joined their mom in the living room.

"I want to talk to you two about work," Mom explained. "We've got a big project that I'm going to manage. It'll require me to work extra hours."

"Is that why you've been getting home later than usual the last few days?" Ebony asked.

"Yes," Mom confirmed. "And I'm going to have to put in even more hours."

"OK," said Ebony. "That's a good opportunity for you, right?"

"It is, and I'm excited about it. But this means I'm going to rely on you two to help around the house a bit more. It'll be an adjustment, I know. But we'll get through this."

***

TALK ABOUT IT

- How do you think Ebony felt when she learned that her mom was going to be working more hours than usual?

- Why do you think Mom asked Ebony and Eric to help out more?

- What would you do if your parent asked you to do more at home? How would you feel?

The rest of
the week and
the next week
were the same
as always.
That Saturday,
though, the
changes began.

The rest of the week and the next week were the same as always. That Saturday, though, the changes began. Ebony had a soccer game. Her mom cheered her on as usual, but she was there for only the first half. She couldn't stay for the entire game because she had to go to work. It was the first time Ebony could remember that her mom wasn't there for the whole game.

The adjustments Mom said they would have to make continued. Mom texted Ebony on Tuesday afternoon to say she was working late and might not be home until eight or nine o'clock. After soccer practice, Ebony hurried home to make dinner for her brother.

"Eric," Ebony called as she walked through the door, "I'm home."

"Hey," he said.

"Hey," Ebony replied. "How was school today? Do you have any homework?"

"Fine," he said. "Yeah, just some math problems."

"Great," said Ebony. "Get your homework and come to the kitchen. You can work on it while I make dinner."

"Where's Mom?" he asked.

"She has to work late again," Ebony replied. "It's just you and me tonight."

"What are you going to make?" Eric asked.

"What day is it?" she replied.

"Tuesday," Eric said, his face lighting up. "Taco Tuesday!"

"Yep," said Ebony, smiling back. "Now, go get your homework. I can help you if you need it, but I know you're a wiz at math."

"Why, yes, yes I am," Eric said, taking off down the hallway to his room.

***

TALK ABOUT IT

- How would you feel if your parent or guardian had to miss your soccer game or something similar?
- Do you think Ebony's mom is handling the situation well? Why or why not?

Ebony made tacos and checked Eric's homework. They ate together at the kitchen table, not in the dining room, where they usually ate with their mom. Eating in the dining room wasn't the same without Mom there. After dinner, while Eric loaded the dishwasher, Ebony gathered the laundry and took it to the basement. She sorted the clothes as her mom had taught her and then started a load. Next, she went to the living room, grabbing her backpack along the way. She had her own math problems to solve. By that time, Eric had planted himself in front of the TV.

Seven o'clock came and went, and then eight. By then, Ebony had finished her homework and had taken over the couch. Eric had gone to his room to play video games. At nine o'clock, Ebony checked on Eric.

"Hey," said Ebony. "You may want to think about going to bed soon."

"But Mom isn't home yet," Eric replied. "I want to say good night to her."

"I know, but I don't know when she'll be home," Ebony explained. "When she texted me this afternoon, she said she'd be home by eight or nine, and it's nine now." Ebony paused, thinking about what to do next.

"How 'bout we send her a text?" Ebony proposed. "She may not see it right away because she's busy, but she'll know we're thinking about her."

"OK, yeah, that sounds good," said Eric.

Ebony felt anxious. She wasn't used to all this responsibility.

Ebony grabbed her phone and took a selfie with Eric. They made funny faces, hoping it would make their mom laugh. Ebony sent the photo with a short text: "Hi! We miss you."

Ebony left Eric to his game and headed back to the living room. She started dozing off when she remembered the laundry. She headed to the basement and changed loads. Climbing the stairs, she remembered lunch. She needed to make all three of their lunches for tomorrow. Ebony felt anxious. She wasn't used to all this responsibility. There was just so much to do. It felt like a weight on her shoulders. She wanted her mom, and she hoped things would be back to normal soon.

TALK ABOUT IT

- Why do you think Ebony was stressed?
- What could Eric have done to help more?
- What advice would you offer Ebony to help her deal with the stress?

39

ASK THE

EXPERT

Stress within the family is unavoidable. It happens to everyone at some point, whether from situations big or small. Dealing with stress together as a family can help strengthen those family bonds. But even when families are working together, anyone can feel anxious and get overwhelmed, especially when responsibilities are piled on. When faced with stress, you may not be able to change the situation, but you can take steps to care for yourself.

Pay attention to how you're feeling, including how you're doing physically and emotionally. Are you low on energy? Are you feeling impatient and frustrated—not yourself? These are some signs that you're stressed. You can combat stress in different ways, such as by getting enough rest and by being active. Try to find time to do things you enjoy. These things will help balance feelings of anxiety and being overwhelmed. You can work with your family to lessen your stress as well. Share your feelings with them, and keep that communication open. Find time for family activities, even if they're as simple as a movie night. And if any burden seems too big to bear, share the load. See whether other family members can take over some of your responsibilities.

GET **HEALTHY**

- Think of ways you can help when a family situation takes one or both parents away from their usual family commitments.

- When helping with things your parents usually do, simply try your best. If you don't know how to do something, ask an adult to show you how.

- Make a to-do list and prioritize the items. If some things can wait, let them wait to avoid getting overwhelmed.

- Take care of yourself. That means keeping up with school as best you can, getting enough sleep, exercising, spending time with friends, and finding downtime.

- Share your experience with someone you trust.

THE LAST WORD FROM **BECCA**

Taking on additional responsibilities at home can be difficult, even overwhelming. That's especially true because you don't have control over the situation—you can't make it go away. When I was 15, my mom left. My older brother and my sister were already out of the house. I started doing the laundry, making dinner regularly, and looking after my younger brother. I don't think I thought twice about it. I just did it.

I remember my sister being at the house one time when I was doing laundry. I was folding towels. She said I was doing it wrong. She was wrong. The towels got folded, and that's what mattered. Do your best, and if you get stressed, tell your parents or another adult relative. Tell your favorite teacher. Talk to your school counselor. Expressing your feelings will help you get through tough times.

CHAPTER FOUR

WEARING MAKEUP

S upport and guidance are a big part of being in a family. Parents should help their children, teach them, and cheer them on. Sometimes, though, that doesn't happen—at least not initially. As much as we may hope our parents will know the answers to everything, that isn't always the case. In some instances, our parents simply don't have experience with what we're going through.

Navigating adolescence can be difficult for kids and parents alike. This can be particularly so for families with a single father and a daughter. While families with a single mom are common, those with single dads are much less so. Single dads face a variety of challenges. Some of them are gender specific, such as struggling to talk to their daughters about menstruation. That may challenge single dads because they lack the perspective a mother has. As a single dad, Sasha's father was entering new territory when Sasha said she wanted to wear makeup.

And Sasha had to figure out how to communicate what she needed to her dad.

SASHA'S STORY

Sasha held still while Anika applied the colorful powder to her eyelids. Sasha was hanging out with her two best friends, Anika and Hana, at Anika's house. They were waiting for pizza to arrive, so they figured they would pass the time by putting on makeup. Actually, they decided Anika would put makeup on Sasha and Hana. Anika had been wearing makeup for a while and was really good at it. At 15 years old, Sasha hadn't been interested in makeup much, but she played along. The girls talked and laughed as Anika pretended to be a makeup artist. She picked out some wild, bright colors—even some glitter. Sasha wasn't so sure she liked the colors, but they were just having fun. The evening flew by. At nine o'clock, Anika's mom drove Sasha home.

Sasha walked through the front door with a hello. She lived with her dad. When Sasha was 13, her mom left. Sasha's mom was only 17 when she'd had Sasha. When her mom turned 30, she decided she wanted to be on her own. Just like that, Sasha's world changed. She had always spent every other weekend with her dad, but now she lived with him all the time. One thing that helped Sasha cope with her mom leaving was spending time with her friends.

Sasha's mom was only 17 when she'd had Sasha. When her mom turned 30, she decided she wanted to be on her own.

TALK ABOUT IT

- What might it be like to lose a family member or someone close to you unexpectedly?
- What do you think Sasha thought and felt after moving to her dad's?
- Sasha coped by spending time with her friends. What are some other ways someone could cope with a parent leaving?

"Hey, how was your night?" Sasha's dad asked as he headed her way from the living room. "Did you have fun?"

"It was good," she said. She started talking about her day at school and her evening at Anika's. Then her dad got to where Sasha was standing.

"Are you wearing makeup?" he asked.

"Oh, yeah," she said, forgetting she had makeup on. "Isn't it fun?"

Sasha's dad stood there looking at her. He didn't say anything.

"What's the matter?" she asked.

"I just . . . I . . . I didn't expect you to be wearing makeup," he said. "I've never seen you with it on before. I'm surprised."

"Do you like it?" Sasha asked.

Sasha's dad wasn't sure what to say. "Well," he replied, taking a breath, "I think it might be a bit much."

"Oh," Sasha said, her smile disappearing. She suddenly felt very self-conscious about the makeup. "Well, I have some homework to do, so I'm going to work on it." She made her way past her dad and ran up the stairs. Instead of going to her room, though, Sasha went to the bathroom and shut the door.

Sasha looked at herself in the mirror, at the colorful smoky eye shadow Anika had applied. Her eyeliner was intense, and the mascara was slightly clumped. She barely recognized herself, but she didn't hate it either. Then she thought about her dad's face when he looked at her. Her eyes began welling with tears. She wiped them away but smudged the makeup across her face. She tried to rub it away with her hand, but that only made it worse. She grabbed a

TALK ABOUT IT

- Why do you think Sasha felt self-conscious about the makeup?

- Imagine you're Sasha's dad. How might you have responded when seeing your daughter in makeup unexpectedly and for the first time?

washcloth, ran it under hot water, and began furiously scrubbing the smeared makeup.

She heard a knock at the door.

"Sasha, are you OK? May I come in?" her dad asked.

Sasha didn't respond right away. "Yeah," she said.

Dad opened the door. Sasha was standing at the sink with a washcloth covered in smudges of black, bright pink, and purple. Black was smeared under her eyes. Sasha didn't want to look at him.

"Hey," he said.

"Hey," Sasha echoed back.

"You didn't do anything wrong, Sasha," he told her.

"But you didn't like my makeup," she said.

"Sweetie, I didn't expect to see you in makeup," he explained. "I was really surprised. And, well, you left me speechless. My little girl isn't a little girl anymore. I didn't know how to respond. I didn't mean to hurt your feelings. I'm sorry."

"It's OK," Sasha said. "The other girls at school wear makeup. Anika wears makeup, and I wanted to try it." Sasha paused. "And Mom would wear makeup. When I was little, she would put lip gloss on me. She told me when I turned 13, I could start wearing makeup. She said she would teach me. But then she left, and I didn't really care about makeup anymore."

"I didn't know she made that promise to you."

"She did," said Sasha, scrubbing at her face. "And I want to wear makeup now . . . but not so much or so bright."

> "Sweetie, I didn't expect to see you in makeup," he explained. "I was really surprised."

"OK," he replied. "Be gentle. You're going to rub your cheeks raw." Dad stepped closer and held out his hand over the sink. "Here, let me help."

Sasha's dad got the wet washcloth sudsy and then handed it back to her. She took the soapy cloth and started to wash her face. The rest of the makeup started to come off.

"You good?" he asked.

"Yeah," Sasha replied, looking in the mirror and focusing on her face.

***

TALK ABOUT IT

- Why was it important for Sasha to say she wanted to wear makeup?
- Do you think it was helpful for Sasha to talk about her mom? Why or why not?
- Why do you think Sasha was surprised by her dad?
- Has anyone done something for you that was unexpected? What did that feel like?

A few days later, after eating dinner and doing the dishes, Sasha's dad called her upstairs. She found him in the bathroom, his laptop set up on the counter.

"What are you doing?" Sasha asked.

"It's time for a makeup lesson," he replied.

On the counter was mascara, lip gloss, and a few colors of eye shadow. Sasha's dad had stopped at a beauty store on the way home from work. He had shown a picture of Sasha to a clerk, who helped him pick out items.

"What? Really?" Sasha said, surprised.

"Definitely," he said. "I learned while shopping today that lots of tutorials are available online. I have one ready to go." Sasha's dad grabbed one of her headbands. He pulled it over his head, then up to pull his hair off his face.

"OK . . ." Sasha said, drawing the word out, a bit unsure of what her dad was up to. "What are you doing?"

"I'm going to do it with you," he said.

"You are not," Sasha said. "You're playing with me."

"No, really," her dad said, unwrapping some mascara. "We're going to do this together, starting with some eye basics. Which eye shadow do you want to use first?"

Sasha picked up a pale pink that shimmered.

"Good choice," he said. "Are you ready?"

"I'm ready," Sasha said, moving close to her dad to watch the video.

Dad took a deep breath. "OK," he said, and pressed play.

ASK THE
EXPERT

Adolescence can be challenging, and not just for kids. Sasha's dad didn't know how best to handle his daughter's wearing makeup or how to help her learn about applying it. But Sasha faced the issue of makeup head-on. She could have chosen to not say anything, especially because the topic was painful. Instead, she was open about her feelings and her experience with her mom. As a result, Sasha got the support she wanted and needed from her dad. Even better, doing online makeup tutorials together strengthened their relationship.

Whether you have one parent or two, there are bound to be moments of conflict as you grow up. Do your best to tell your parent what you want and how you feel, no matter how big or small a topic may seem. You can plan what you'll talk about ahead of time. Or you can be brave in the moment and respectfully share your thoughts. Some topics may seem awkward or uncomfortable. But it's important to speak up anyway. If you don't, your parent can't understand your experience or help you. Not all parents will be supportive all the time. You won't know, though, unless you express what you want. And if you aren't getting the support you need, you can seek it from other sources. Talk to other trusted adults, such as other relatives or counselors.

GET **HEALTHY**

- Remember that parents learn as they go. Try to be patient—with your parents and yourself. Sometimes you just have to navigate situations together.

- Be willing to compromise. You may not get all of what you want, but you may get some of it.

- If a parent has said or done something that has hurt your feelings, say something. Sometimes you need to take the lead.

- If you're the daughter of a single dad, you can also reach out to a trusted woman, such as an aunt. She can back up your dad and give you both advice.

THE LAST WORD FROM **BECCA**

Daughters of single dads miss out on having both parents in some situations, such as when a mom would be able to discuss changes that occur during puberty. On the flip side, single dads miss out on having a partner to tackle issues kids face on their way to adulthood. This goes for single moms of sons, too, and all parents in general. Wearing makeup was a milestone for Sasha. Helping Sasha with makeup was a milestone for her dad. He got to see his daughter in a different, more mature light. More than that, he took advantage of the situation to bond with his daughter as a single father. He could have pushed Sasha onto a salesclerk or a female relative for help. Instead, he chose to create a special memory that strengthened his bond with her. When faced with parent-child challenges, do your best to communicate honestly and to give your parent a chance. He or she may surprise you.

CHAPTER FIVE

AN UNRELIABLE PARENT

Families face so many issues. Some are easy to resolve; others are far heavier and more difficult. One issue that can have dramatic and even devastating effects on a family is addiction. Addiction is also known as substance use disorder. Millions of individuals struggle with substance abuse such as alcoholism. And many more who care about those individuals are affected. The effects of addiction on families vary. What substance use disorders have in common is that they're detrimental. Alcohol abuse affects the users' health and well-being. It changes how they behave, which affects their home and work.

Addiction can cause a person to become unpredictable and unreliable. The addiction becomes the main focus of

In serious cases, a parent with substance use disorder can become undependable, leaving children to fend for themselves.

the person's life. Financial problems may result if people with addictions lose their jobs because they were unreliable or if they spend money intended for essentials on drugs or alcohol.

In serious cases, a parent with substance use disorder can become undependable, leaving children to fend for themselves. Some children take on the role of adult and caretaker to make up for the parent. Children of those suffering from addiction may also become hyperalert, never sure of how their parent might behave and what might happen. Conflict can become common, and trust can deteriorate. This was Trina's experience.

TRINA'S STORY

Trina was having a quick breakfast before heading to school. Her mom was getting ready to head to work.

"Trina, before you head out, I want you to know that I have something after work today," said Mom. "I need you to be here with your sister."

"Sure," Trina replied. "Do you know what time you'll be home? I was planning to go to the basketball game with Lola and Molly. Do you think you'll be home in time?"

"I'm sure I will," she said. "It's just a little get-together for a coworker whose last day is today. What time is the game?"

"It's at seven thirty," said Trina, "though we talked about going for pizza first."

"OK," Mom said. "I'll be home by six. Will that work?"

"Definitely," said Trina. "Thanks, Mom."

***

After school, Trina hurried home to be with Kia, her little sister. Kia was 11, and she and Trina got along well. Trina made them a snack. Then she helped Kia clean her guinea pig's cage. When they finished, Trina got ready for the game. She changed into school colors, fixed her hair, and applied some mascara and lip gloss. Then she bounced back into the dining room, happy to be going out with her friends. She looked at her watch. Mom should be home any minute now.

Trina and Kia started watching a movie. Trina kept checking her watch: 5:30, 5:45, 6:00. If her mom didn't walk through the door in the next five minutes, it would be too late to go for pizza before the game.

If her mom didn't walk through the door in the next five minutes, it would be too late to go for pizza before the game.

She texted Lola and Molly and let them know her mom was running late. She couldn't leave Kia alone and would meet them at the game. At seven she told them she wouldn't make it to the game. She went to the kitchen and fixed some dinner for herself and Kia. After eating, they headed back to the couch to watch TV.

Finally, Trina heard the garage door. It took a few minutes before Mom appeared in the kitchen.

"Girls, I'm home," she called.

Trina watched Kia happily greet their mom. Trina wasn't happy and didn't greet her mother. Mom asked how their day was and whether they wanted anything for dinner.

"Mom," said Trina, clearly frustrated, "it's eight thirty. We *had* dinner."

TALK ABOUT IT

= How do you think Trina felt when her mom didn't show up as promised?

= Have you ever had a situation in which a parent or other adult didn't keep a promise? What did that feel like? How did you respond?

"Eight thirty?" Mom asked. "I didn't realize it was so late."

"It is," said Trina. "I missed the game."

"The game?" Mom said softly. "The game! Oh, you were going out with Molly and Lola. Oh, honey, I'm sorry. My work thing went late."

Mom hugged Trina and kissed her on the cheek. Trina could smell alcohol on her mother's breath.

***

On Monday, Trina apologized to her friends for missing the game. They said it was OK. The trio talked about the upcoming week and weekend. They decided they'd meet for breakfast that Saturday at their favorite hangout and then go to an early movie. It was a plan.

Saturday morning, Trina hopped out of bed and got ready. She checked on Kia, who was having a bowl of cereal. When she asked Kia where mom was, Kia said that she was still in bed.

Trina headed to her mom's room. She knocked. No response. She peeked inside. Mom was asleep. Trina walked softly to her mother's bedside. She saw a wine glass on the bedside table. Stepping closer, Trina accidently kicked the wine bottle that was on the floor.

It wasn't the first time her mom had slept in hungover, but it seemed to be happening more and more. One day a few weeks earlier, Trina had struggled to get her mom up for work. Finally, she had called her mom's office, explaining that her mom wasn't feeling well and wouldn't be there that day. Trina hated lying, but she didn't know what else to do. Jackie, the woman Trina spoke with, was very nice. She didn't question Trina. In fact, Jackie said she hoped Trina's mother felt better soon. That didn't make Trina feel better.

Trina was really looking forward to hanging out with Lola and Molly. She didn't want to let them down, especially after missing the game. Trina took a deep breath, unsure of the response she'd get.

"Mom?" she said.

Nothing.

"Mom," Trina repeated, placing her hand on her mom's arm.

Trina's mom made a bit of a noise.

"Mom, it's time to get up," Trina said.

Finally, her mom answered. "What time is it?" she asked. "Am I late for work?"

"No, Mom," Trina responded. "It's Saturday."

"Saturday," she repeated. "Great. I can sleep."

"Mom, I have to go," said Trina, feeling frustrated. "I'm meeting Lola and Molly."

"OK, bye," she said, rolling over, away from Trina. "Have fun. See ya later."

TALK ABOUT IT

= Would you have stayed with Kia or gone out with your friends?

= Why do you think Trina didn't want to leave Kia alone with their mom?

"But Kia's here, Mom," Trina said.

"She'll be fine," Mom replied softly, dozing off.

Trina didn't want to leave Kia, so she decided to text Molly and Lola. Just as she had done when she called her mom's office when her mother wouldn't get up for work, Trina told her friends her mom was sick. Now she was lying to her friends, and she felt terrible doing it. She didn't know what else to do. She wanted to see her friends—to get out of the house and away from her mother—but she didn't want to leave Kia there.

***

As the weeks passed, Trina did her best to keep smiling, but she felt less and less like it. As her mom drank more, Trina felt more responsible for taking care of Kia and taking care of the house—even taking care of her mom. Mom was becoming increasingly unreliable, and Kia wasn't old enough to care for herself. Trina made sure Kia was up and ready for school, fed, and had her homework done. Trina also went online and paid some of the bills. She knew where her mom kept her account information. Bringing in the mail one day after school, Trina saw an envelope with "Final Notice" on it. If the electric bill wasn't paid, the electricity would be turned off.

Trina felt like she was having to be the mom, but she wasn't the mom. And she couldn't seem to help her mom. She was afraid to say what was really happening. She didn't want her mom to get into trouble, but her mom needed help. Trina needed help. She didn't know what to do.

TALK ABOUT IT

- Why do you think Trina chose to not tell the truth about what was going on?

- How might you feel if you had a family member with a substance use disorder?

- Why might asking for help be challenging for a teen with a parent who has a substance abuse problem?

- What do you think Trina should do now?

ASK THE

EXPERT

It is not uncommon for a child to have a parent with an addiction. Millions of Americans struggle with a substance use disorder. Specifically, many of them battle alcoholism. Addiction is a serious matter, causing problems for those with the addiction and for those who are close to them. Living with someone who drinks too much or uses drugs can be painful and stressful. The addicted person can become unpredictable, unreliable, and irresponsible. He or she may seem like another person.

The effects of addiction can be painful and long-lasting. For example, children of those with addictions often suffer from anxiety and depression. Some blame themselves for their parent's behavior. And because many children end up caring for and protecting the parent, these children often limit or even lose contact with the people in their lives who would give them care and support.

If your parent has a problem with alcohol or another substance, know that it's not your fault. You and other family members can try to help the person who has an addiction, but you can't make the person change. The person with an addiction has to choose to get help for himself or herself. Seek help for yourself. Numerous resources are available, including therapists and support groups.

GET **HEALTHY**

- Understand that the situation isn't your fault. You aren't responsible for anyone's behavior, including your family member's substance abuse.

- Let yourself feel. Trying to not feel may seem like a good idea, but it will keep you from getting the support you need.

- Tell someone. Get your feelings, fears, and frustrations out. Talk to a friend or trusted adult. Adults may provide knowledge and support another teen can't. Counselors can help too. They are trained to support people in your situation.

- Find a safe place to go when things become too much. Examples include a relative's or friend's house, a library, or even a movie theater.

THE LAST WORD FROM **BECCA**

Having a family member with an addiction can cause a variety of feelings, including pain, frustration, anxiety, anger, and sadness. One of my family members has an addiction. She's made many poor choices as a result of addiction that hurt her, her children, and our family. For many years, I tried to help her as best I could, such as by babysitting her children when I was a teenager and lending her money. It took me a long time to stop trying to help her. When I think about her, feeling sad is kind of unavoidable, and that's OK. The important thing to remember about addiction is this: as much as you may love and want to help someone with an addiction, that person must take care of himself or herself. You can't do it for that person. Your job is to care for yourself.

CHAPTER SIX

MONEY FEARS

Have you ever given up something, even for just a short time? Imagine giving up something—or several things—as a family to save money. Families might stop eating out, or they might buy generic items instead of brand-name goods because generic goods are usually less expensive. Some families may have to cut back on family outings or cancel kids' activities such as dance classes or music lessons. Imagine doing those things—and more—to survive.

Perhaps one of the most challenging issues any person can face is not having enough money. Not having sufficient funds is a reality for many Americans. In 2019, 40 percent of US families didn't have savings. If an emergency came up, such as a car repair or a trip to the hospital, these families wouldn't be able to pay for it on their own. Even just a few hundred dollars would be unmanageable.

Even if someone has savings, that's no guarantee of stability—at least not indefinitely. What happens when a string of unexpected expenses pop up, draining the money that's in savings? Giving up or cutting back on some things helps. But when in the midst of financial struggle, keeping a positive mindset may be challenging. When her family had to cut back, Genesis had to work with her family to get through the difficult time.

GENESIS'S STORY

It was early March, and Genesis was dreaming about summer. It wasn't because the day was cold and gray and she wanted warm weather and sunshine. She was thinking about her birthday, which was in August. She'd been dreaming about it for longer than she could remember. Birthdays were always special, but this one was going to be extra special. She'd be 15. This summer would be her quinceañera. Genesis's family didn't have much money to spare, but her parents had been carefully saving what they could to create the party Genesis wanted.

Genesis knew her dress alone would be expensive, but her parents had promised to get her the princess-type gown traditionally worn as part of this birthday celebration. Genesis couldn't wait to try on some dresses to find just the right one. She recalled how beautiful her cousin Marisol had been at her quinceañera last year.

Genesis already had a tiara. She would wear her mom's. It was stored safely in her mom's closet. Sometimes, Genesis secretly got it out of the box and tried it on. She was so excited about wearing it on her next birthday.

TALK ABOUT IT

- Why do you think Genesis's family made saving for her quinceañera a priority?

- What cultural celebrations are important to you?

- Have you had an experience in which you were really excited about an upcoming event? What was the event? What made you excited about it?

***

During the month of March, Genesis's family had some unexpected expenses. First, the water heater broke and needed to be replaced immediately. Genesis's parents were able to handle that cost, but a week later, Genesis's dad was in a car accident. A person ran a stop sign and hit his car. Thankfully, her dad was OK. Unfortunately, he had to buy a new car, and there wouldn't be insurance money to help with the cost. Only a few days later, the stove stopped working. Genesis's dad was great at fixing things, but he couldn't repair that. The stove, like the water heater, was old. They could use their microwave for a while, but Genesis's mom insisted on getting a new stove.

During the month of March, Genesis's family had some unexpected expenses.

Each of these events was unexpected, and all of them were costly, especially the car. Then, making matters worse, Genesis's mom got the flu and had to miss a week of work. Because she was paid by the hour and had only two sick days, that meant no income for three days. Even worse, Genesis's mom had gotten so dehydrated, she ended up in urgent care. That left the family with a bill for costs not covered by their health insurance.

Genesis knew that these things had been hard on her parents. She would see them staying up late talking quietly at the kitchen table, looking tired and serious. But her parents had also tried to keep her and her brother from worrying, so life went on as usual—more or less. Genesis didn't totally grasp her family's situation until she noticed some changes at home.

For the first time in years, they didn't order pizza on Friday night. Pizza on Friday had become part of the family's routine. She also noticed the house was chilly. When Genesis went to turn up the heat, her mother told her not to and said to put on a sweater or hoodie.

"What's going on?" Genesis asked. "Why can't I turn up the heat?"

"We're just trying to save money where we can," her mother explained.

"Why?"

Her mom paused for a moment. "We didn't want to worry you."

"Worry me?" Genesis replied. "About what?"

Her mom took a deep breath and then asked Genesis to sit on the couch with her.

"We're struggling, Genesis. Finances are tight."

"Because of the car and appliances, right?" Genesis asked.

"Yes, exactly. We're being extra careful with spending. We're trying to save in any way we can."

"I get it," Genesis said. "Thanks for telling me what's going on. I'll put on some socks and a cardigan."

"I can fix you some hot chocolate," Mom offered. "We even have mini marshmallows."

"Sure," Genesis replied. "I'd like that."

Genesis took the hot chocolate to her room to do her homework, but she found focusing difficult. Genesis was glad her mom was open with her, but now she worried what would happen next. How long would they have to cut back? *Will we have enough money for my quinceañera?* she thought.

At dinner that night, Genesis's dad talked about what was going on financially. He told Genesis and Jorge, her brother, that they would all have to contribute to cutting back on spending.

"That means bundling up when it's chilly because we're not going to crank up the heat," Mom said.

"And taking shorter showers," Dad added. "We need to work together to get through this. And we *will* get through this," Dad said emphatically.

***

The family members did what they could to save money. They clipped coupons and changed their cable package. They stopped eating out. Genesis knew her parents were working hard to make up for the savings the family had spent on the car and other recent expenses. She wondered whether she should get a part-time job. Her mom told her no and said to concentrate on school. But she couldn't focus. And dreams of her quinceañera

Genesis was glad her mom was open with her, but now she worried what would happen next. How long would they have to cut back?

TALK ABOUT IT

■ What do you think it was like for Genesis to sense something was going on and not know the facts?

■ How might cutting back affect family life, practically and emotionally?

were fading. What if something else happened that required a lot of money? How would her family make it?

Genesis's worry began to show. She became quiet at home. And her performance in school declined. She got a C on a biology test. It was the first C she had ever gotten. Her biology teacher asked her to stay after class. After a few questions, the teacher

got to the heart of the problem. She also learned that Genesis hadn't talked to her parents about her concerns.

"I think you should talk to your parents about what you're feeling," Ms. Colter said. "They need to know what you're thinking and feeling so they can help."

"OK," Genesis sighed, feeling a bit better for saying out loud the worry she'd been keeping inside. "I will."

TALK ABOUT IT

= How might you react to hearing your family was struggling financially and you had to cut back on your usual spending?

= Why do you think it was difficult for Genesis to focus on her schoolwork?

= Why do you think Ms. Colter told Genesis to talk to her parents? What advice would you give her?

ASK THE
EXPERT

The situation Genesis's family experienced is very common, especially during a recession. But people can struggle financially anytime. Having unexpected expenses can affect a family's financial security. The family may change the way they eat and live. In the extreme, the result could be a lack of food and shelter.

But a family's financial insecurity can have even more effects, including on physical health and mental health. For example, ongoing worry about finances has been connected to migraines and sleep problems. And families that are struggling financially are less likely than financially secure families to seek medical or dental care when needed. They are also less likely to get medicines that have been prescribed. In addition, parental stress can cause stress in children and have negative results, such as mental illness.

Communication about what's going on and what everyone is feeling is one way to get through the situation. Talk with each other. Your family can also reach out to extended family or friends for support. And resources such as food pantries are available to help your family get through difficult times and meet your basic needs.

GET HEALTHY

- Trust that things will get better. All families go through rough patches.

- Have your family brainstorm possibilities for saving money and making money. Set financial goals and work on them as a family.

- Explore resources such as food pantries and, if your family is struggling with debt, credit counselors. Asking for help is OK.

- Try to be positive. Doing things as a family that you enjoy, such as game night, will take your minds off the situation and help you fight the worry.

- Share your concerns with your parents, and ask them to be open about what's going on.

THE LAST WORD FROM BECCA

As a freelancer, I have often found my work and finances to be unpredictable. When I start worrying about money, I can quickly go downhill, fearing the worst. When that happens, I do my best to focus on the now and what I can control, such as cutting back on spending, looking for work, and not getting sucked into worrying about what might happen. Sometimes, I ask my parents for help. I feel a bit like a failure when I do, thinking I shouldn't have to because I'm an adult, but I feel better getting their help. And when I'm doing OK and have a friend or family member in need, I offer help to that person.

CHAPTER SEVEN

A SAFE PLACE

Family relationships are some of our most important relationships. They are our first relationships. Ideally, our parents provide us with food and shelter and clothing. More than that, they love and care for us. They cheer us on. Together, these things combine to create a sense of safety. We develop trust in our parents and other family members. Trust binds a family's members. Trust helps us feel like we belong to our family. But we don't always have that trust we hope for.

Many children face a different experience with their parents. For various reasons, their parents don't provide a safe place. In 2017, almost 700,000 children were in foster care for at least part of the year. Foster children don't live with their biological parents, and some may be separated from their siblings as well. Some foster kids end up in good homes for a long time. Some move from home to home. Others may live in an institution or

a group home. For many foster kids, trusting others can be difficult. Mia knew that firsthand.

MIA'S STORY

Mia was 17 and had been in and out of foster homes since she was six years old. The longest she'd lived anywhere was nine months. Mia longed for a place to call home and a space that was just hers. More than that, she wanted parents she could talk to and rely on. But she didn't really let herself dream of that anymore. She had lived in so many different houses over the past 11 years. Most were OK, and one or two were good. Some, though, were not. The adults weren't very nice. They yelled at her and the other foster kids living with them. She didn't know why these people even wanted her there. They didn't seem to like kids. She had learned to keep to herself and try to be invisible. Even in the good homes, she didn't really let people in because she was sure she'd end up moving. Moving was what she knew, so it was what she came to expect.

Mia was moving again, this time to live with the Kennedys. Her caseworker brought her to yet another house to meet yet another couple.

TALK ABOUT IT

▪ Have you ever wanted a space of your own? What was it like to have that desire?

▪ What challenges do you think foster kids face?

"Mia, we're so happy to have you here," said Marie, her new foster mother. "You can call me Marie. And this is Tina, my wife."

"Hi, Mia," said Tina. "We're so glad to meet you."

"And this is Charlie," said Marie, patting the golden retriever standing next to her. "He's super friendly. He may just knock you over with his tail once it starts wagging."

Marie took Mia to her bedroom. Tina and Charlie followed. It had a bed, dresser, and desk. It even had a computer and a TV. A window seat was filled with all kinds of pillows in different colors. Tina told Mia that they could paint the room and get new bedding to match her style. Tina and Marie wanted her to feel at home with them.

That first day with the Kennedys went so much better than Mia had dared to hope. It ended with Mia watching TV in her room. Charlie was even there, snuggled up next to her. She wasn't fighting over the TV with anyone or having to break up kids from fighting with each other. It was peaceful and quiet. As she dozed off, Mia wondered how long it would be before it ended.

***

As the weeks passed, Mia felt more at home. She was settling in at school and adjusting to her new routine. Mia told Marie and Tina about some of her experiences as a foster kid, including some painful ones. At one house, some other children were playing in the house and broke a crystal vase. They threw away the pieces. When the foster mother realized the vase was missing, the kids blamed Mia, saying she stole it. The couple didn't want to hear anything Mia had to say. The foster parents believed the kids and made the authorities take Mia away.

Marie and Tina seemed to trust Mia. They let her be at the house by herself every day after school and simply asked that she text them when she got home so they knew she was OK. She was glad they trusted her.

TALK ABOUT IT

= What might Mia have been thinking or feeling when she met the Kennedys?

= How do you think you would feel if you were Mia?

As the weeks passed, Mia felt more at home.

***

One day, when Mia was at her desk doing homework, Charlie came into her room. He had his favorite ball. Mia took the ball and gave it a little throw. Charlie grabbed it and brought it right back. "Good boy," Mia said, taking the ball and patting him on

the head. "OK, buddy, I have to get my homework done, so just one more."

Mia grabbed the ball and threw it, but her aim was off, and she threw it harder than she had intended. The ball hit a picture on the wall. It was a photo of Tina and Marie on their wedding day. The photo crashed to the floor. The frame and its glass broke. It was such an important picture. Marie had told Mia that the elaborate frame was a gift from Tina's parents.

Mia panicked. She picked up the picture. Tina and Marie looked so happy. They wouldn't be happy when they saw what she had done. Her experiences had taught her to be guarded and to expect the worst. At worst they were going to make her leave over this. At best they wouldn't trust her anymore.

Mia took the picture in its broken frame and slid it under her bed. Next, Mia went to her closet and got out the bag she had all her belongings in when she moved in. She put it on her bed and then grabbed some clothes and put them in it. She couldn't stand to think of Marie and Tina's disappointment.

I gotta go, Mia thought. *They're gonna be so mad. They'll hate me. They'll make me leave just like the Franklins did.* Mia was so focused on packing that she didn't hear Marie come home. Mia jumped at the sound of Marie's voice.

Mia panicked. She picked up the picture. Tina and Marie looked so happy. They wouldn't be happy when they saw what she had done.

"Hi," said Marie. "What are you doing? What's going on?"

Mia froze. She stood there, head down. "I'm sorry, Marie. I'm so sorry," she cried. Mia got down on the floor, reached under the bed, and pulled out the picture and broken frame. She explained that she had been playing with Charlie and broke it.

"I shouldn't have been playing with him with his ball inside, I know. I'm so sorry. I'm so, *so* sorry."

85

By then, Tina had come home, too, and she was standing in the doorway to Mia's room.

"You're packing because of a broken picture frame?" Marie asked.

"Yes," Mia sniffled.

"Oh, Mia, it's only a frame," said Marie, handing it to Tina.

"We may be able to get this fixed," Tina said. "And even if the frame can't be fixed, we can just replace it. You certainly don't need to leave."

Marie sat down on Mia's bed. "Here, sit," she said, patting the bed. Mia sat down.

"Mia, we want you here," said Marie. "We're so glad you're here."

Mia looked at Tina, then Marie. She could hardly believe it. They weren't going to send her away. More than that, they wanted her there.

Marie took Mia's hands in her own. "Look at me," she said. "I'll tell you this as often as you need or want to hear it: We want you here. We're happy you're here."

"And we're not going anywhere," added Tina. "Give us time and you'll see that."

Mia wiped the tears from her cheeks.

"And next time something like this happens," said Marie, "please just talk to us. OK?"

"OK," said Mia, letting out a sigh of relief.

"Why don't you put that bag away," said Marie. "And if you want to join us downstairs for dinner, we'll be there."

TALK ABOUT IT

- Have you ever accidently broken something important? What happened? How did you react? Why did you react that way?

- Do you think Marie's and Tina's reactions affected Mia's feelings of safety and trust? How so?

Trust is critical to having successful, happy, and productive relationships. Those include relationships with friends, teachers, coaches, partners, bosses, and families. Trust has several important elements. Reliability is one of them. Mia learned that she could rely on Marie and Tina—and not merely for food and shelter. They were kind and supportive. Sincerity is another element. Marie and Tina were genuine in their care for her. They wanted Mia there, and they showed it in their words and actions. They were also fair and open—two more important qualities that build trust. They didn't punish Mia for breaking the picture frame. It was only a picture frame, and they were clear about that. Also, they were honest about their feelings, affirming they really wanted her there. In turn, Mia also came to trust Marie and Tina. She shared her own feelings with them. It took time, but eventually Mia felt that she could be vulnerable with her foster parents. Together, these pieces helped build trust between Mia and her foster parents and ultimately strengthen their relationship.

GET HEALTHY

- When trust is lacking or has been broken, share your feelings. Perhaps there has been a misunderstanding that can easily be resolved. Or you may help the person who damaged your trust understand what you're feeling so you both can make amends.

- Be open and honest. Let yourself be vulnerable, and let others be vulnerable with you.

- Give as well as take. Trust requires balance. Both people have to share.

- Be reliable. Be true to your word, and follow through on promises.

THE LAST WORD FROM BECCA

Having trust in a new situation or opening yourself up can be difficult, especially if you've had experiences in your life that shook your trust or caused you pain. I was really shy growing up. In high school and college, I didn't have many friends. It was partly because I didn't trust people. My family experiences had taught me not to trust. I was afraid to be hurt, so I wouldn't open myself up to people. I wouldn't let myself be vulnerable. I did the opposite and closed myself off to people and to experiences. And that's the challenge we face once trust is broken: learning to trust again. Do your best to open up and try to trust. If you don't, your self-protection may leave you alone and closed off from the world.

CHAPTER EIGHT

DON'T GO

When you're young and have siblings, you really don't think about them not being part of your life. Perhaps your brother leaves his shoes in the middle of the floor, interrupts you when you're talking to your parents or friends, or sometimes just plain gets in the way. Maybe your sister hogs the bathroom or TV—or both—or she seems to always elbow you at the dinner table. I know my siblings did some of these things.

You likely don't think of things being any other way. I think this can be especially true of having older siblings because they've always been part of your life. For many people, their sibling relationships will probably be the longest relationships they have. Eventually, though, the children in a family usually leave home. And that change can be challenging for those left behind, especially younger siblings. When Sarah's older brother enlisted in the military, Sarah had to face the fact that her brother wasn't going to be around much anymore.

SARAH'S STORY

Sarah had always looked up to Dan, her older brother. Dan was tall and strong. He played sports. He would act silly to make her laugh. Dan liked to bike, hike, and camp. He even pitched a tent in their backyard and let her play in it. And Dan liked birds. His friends didn't really know that, but Sarah knew. Dan shared that love with her, teaching her the names of the different birds that would visit their yard.

TALK ABOUT IT

= If you have siblings, do you look up to them? Or do they look up to you? Why or why not?

= If you don't have a sibling, what might it be like to have one?

Dan was three years older than Sarah. When he got his driver's license, he started taking Sarah to her piano lesson each Saturday. Sometimes, he'd take her for ice cream. "C'mon, Rah-rah," he'd say. That was his nickname for Sarah. Only he called her that, and she loved it. She loved him. He was her big brother, and she knew she could count on him to always be there.

***

The summer before Sarah started ninth grade, Dan got a job. Sarah saw Dan less. Sometimes, he wasn't even home when she went to bed. But he still took Sarah to her piano lesson on Saturdays. She looked forward to hearing those words: "C'mon, Rah-rah, let's go." But even their Saturday routine had changed. As soon as the lesson was over, they'd hurry home. One day, Sarah asked, "Are we going for ice cream today?"

"Sorry," Dan said. "I can't today. I have to be at work in half an hour, so I'm just going to drop you off. But we'll go soon."

"OK," she replied with a sigh.

Dan pulled into their driveway and stopped the car. "OK, here you go," he said. "I'll see ya later, alligator."

"OK," was all Sarah replied.

"A-hem," Dan said. "See you later, alligator."

TALK ABOUT IT

- **Have you ever had an older sibling who's not around as much as before or a sibling who's not available to do things with you? How did it make you feel?**

- **What are some ways Sarah could connect with her brother even though he's busy?**

Sarah couldn't help but smile. "After a while, crocodile," she said back.

Dan backed out of their driveway and drove away. Sarah watched the car go down the street. She wished she were in it and that they were going for ice cream.

***

Summer seemed to fly by, and then it was back to school. Dan kept working even after school started. Fall quickly turned to winter. When spring came, Sarah's family planned a big party. Dan was a senior and was going to graduate. It was a time for celebration. But a big change was ahead as well. Dan was going to leave two weeks after graduation. He had enlisted in the military. His graduation party would also be a going-away party. In two months, he would be gone. Sarah had known for months that Dan would be leaving. He would talk about it at dinner sometimes, but she hadn't wanted to think about it.

One night during dinner, Dan talked about going to California. That's where he would go for boot camp, his initial training. Sarah didn't want to listen.

"May I be excused?" she asked, though she didn't wait for a response. She just walked away and went to her room.

Sarah closed the door. She wasn't sure what to do. She paced for a minute, then sat down. She just stared at the wall, trying to process the idea of Dan moving to California.

There was a soft knock on her door.

"Rah-rah, may I come in?" Dan asked.

Sarah let out a big sigh. "Sure."

Dan sat down next to Sarah. "Hi," he said.

Sarah closed
the door. She
wasn't sure
what to do.

"Hi," she said back. "I don't want you to go."

"Yeah, I get that," Dan said. He paused. "It's part of growing up. You'll move away someday too. In a few years, you'll probably go away to some fancy university, you brainiac."

Sarah smirked. "Yeah, I suppose."

Dan told Sarah why joining the military was important to him. Their father had done it—and their grandfather too. "It's kind of a legacy in our family," he said. "Remember those pictures of Dad and Grandpa in uniform?"

Sarah remembered. Dan also explained that he wanted to defend their country and help people in other countries. And he would get to travel. "Imagine all the new birds I'll see."

Sarah could tell joining the military was important to Dan. Still, she didn't feel better. She started to cry.

"I don't want you to leave me," she said.

Dan wrapped his arms around her just as he did when she was little and afraid of thunder. "Hey," he said, "it'll be OK. You'll be OK. I'm not leaving you for good. Things are just changing. We'll talk on the phone and through video chat like we do with Grandma and Grandpa when they go to Florida for the winter. And I'll come home sometimes. That's all good, right?"

"Yeah," she said, though she wasn't convinced.

"I'm leaving home, but you'll always have me," Dan said. "We'll always be siblings. You can always count on me. And I bet when we're old, I'll probably still call you Rah-rah."

Sarah laughed. "Yeah, probably."

"Are we good?" asked Dan.

"Yeah, we're good," Sarah replied, though she still felt sad.

"Good," Dan said. "Let's go get some dessert. I think I saw a chocolate cake in the kitchen."

***

Two months later, the family had the party and celebrated Dan. Two days after that, Mom, Dad, and Sarah took Dan to the airport so he could fly to California. Dan hugged Dad, then Mom, and then Sarah. She didn't want to let go, but she had to and did. She was quiet on the ride home, sad and unsure of what life without Dan would be like.

At first, Sarah didn't think of Dan as gone. He was just away for a few days, like when he'd go camping for a weekend. But then Saturday came. It was time to go to her piano lesson, and Dan wasn't there to take her. Sarah felt sad sometimes because she missed her big brother, but time made things better—and so did talking to him every few weeks. Dan told her about his new experiences, and Sarah talked about school and piano and whatever came to mind. Dan left home, but he didn't leave her. And knowing that made his being away easier to deal with.

TALK ABOUT IT

- What might it be like to have a sibling move away?

- How might a person adjust to a family member leaving?

- What advice would you give to Sarah to help her cope with missing her brother?

ASK THE
EXPERT

A sibling leaving—whatever the reason—is a big change for a family. It affects the family dynamic. A person will no longer be there, and the family will have to adjust. Additionally, as in Sarah's case, the departure might leave younger siblings feeling abandoned.

Adjusting to change—especially such a big change—can be difficult and take time. And feeling sad is normal. Do your best to be patient with yourself and your sibling who has moved away. If he or she doesn't respond right away when you text or email, be careful not to take it personally. Remember, your brother or sister is starting a new life and has responsibilities. Your sibling is also likely struggling too. It's his or her first time away from home. Your sibling could be feeling all kinds of things, including sadness because he or she misses you. You'll both get through the change, and you'll have all kinds of stories to share when you talk. You may also discover just how much you mean to one another.

GET **HEALTHY**

- Know that it's OK to feel sad and miss your family members.

- Be patient. You'll find a new routine as your family adjusts to the change.

- Share the little things with your sibling. Talk about what you did that day. Share something you learned at school. These small details will help you and your sibling feel like you're part of each other's lives.

- Another way to connect with your sibling is through photos and videos. They provide even more detail about your life and communicate information that words sometimes can't.

THE LAST WORD FROM **BECCA**

When I was between the ages of 12 and 15, half my family left: a brother, my sister, and then my mom. My older brother was the first to leave when he joined the US Marines. That may have been the toughest for me. A family member hadn't moved away before. And being in the military, my brother could have been sent to a dangerous area, which added a layer of worry to the situation.

When a sibling leaves, do what you can to stay connected. My brother would call on holidays, even when he was stationed in another country. I remember being excited about talking to him. And it was great to have him home on leave. When a sibling moves away, our personal world may change, but that doesn't mean the world stops turning or life ends. Our challenge is to adjust—and that can take time. Even when we get used to a new family norm, we may miss our sibling. The best we can do is just keep going. Life without that sibling won't be the same, but it can still be good.

A SECOND
LOOK

As these stories have demonstrated, being part of a family isn't always easy. But you probably knew that already. A grandparent might say no to something you really want. A parent could be unreliable, or you might get a stepparent. You might have money worries or be reluctant to trust. Your older siblings might move away. You've maybe experienced one or more of these situations, and you've certainly experienced a situation with your family that created conflict of some sort.

Whatever tough situations you and your family face—and you'll undoubtedly face a few—they will be opportunities to learn about yourself and your family members. Tough situations may not seem like opportunities initially, but when you step back and do your best to not let emotions take over, you may see that they are. Or maybe you'll realize it later when thinking back on the experiences.

Your interactions with your family prepare you for socializing in the world, with classmates and teammates or teachers and beyond. Eventually, you may find yourself with a partner and children. Here, in your new family, you'll get to face family issues with a wealth of perspective and experience.

Families aren't perfect. Family members make mistakes. Sometimes those mistakes leave us with pain and issues that can last into adulthood. My family continues to challenge me and provide learning opportunities, each time offering me the chance to strengthen my communication and coping skills.

I hope you approach family challenges—now and as an adult—fearlessly. Push yourself to move past your fears, to speak up, and to share what you're thinking and feeling. You can do it. And you'll come out the other side that much stronger.

XOXO,
BECCA

PAY IT

FORWARD

Handling family challenges takes courage, trust, and communication. Discovering what makes you feel your best is a journey that changes throughout your life. Now that you know what to focus on, you can pay it forward to a friend too. Remember the Get Healthy tips throughout this book, and then take these steps to get healthy and get going.

1. Before having an important discussion, make a list of talking points, and think about how you'll respond if the talk doesn't go the way you hope it will.

2. Be respectful, even if you're frustrated. If necessary, excuse yourself from the situation so you don't say or do something to make the situation worse.

3. When you're feeling stressed, take care of yourself. Get enough sleep, get exercise, do things that bring you joy, and do your best to keep up in school.

4. Try to be positive, even during the toughest times.

5. Say something to your family members if they hurt your feelings. Sometimes you need to take the lead.

6. Be patient with your family members. They don't have all the answers. You may have to navigate situations together.

7. Reach out for help when you need to. School counselors and therapists can help individuals and families navigate a variety of situations, and food shelves are one resource for families who need support when facing financial insecurity.

8. Talk. Whatever you may be feeling—stressed, overwhelmed, afraid, sad—tell someone. Depending on the situation, share what's going on with a friend, an adult relative, a teacher, or a therapist.

9. Realize that no family is perfect and that every family faces challenges.

10. If you're taking on new responsibilities around the house and don't know how to do something, ask a parent for help and do your best.

GLOSSARY

addiction
A compulsive need for a habit-forming substance, such as nicotine or alcohol.

adolescence
The period between childhood and adulthood when a young person grows up, beginning at the onset of puberty.

anxiety
A feeling of fear about a future event.

cope
To deal with a personal issue or overcome a difficulty.

detrimental
Harmful.

enlist
To voluntarily join the military.

exacerbate
To make worse.

family dynamic
The typical way members of a family interact.

financial security
The ability to consistently pay for basic needs and work toward financial goals.

foster care
Care provided for a child by someone who is not the parents and who is usually determined by a state authority.

obligations
Responsibilities a person must fulfill.

recession
A period of negative economic growth and, usually, low demand for goods and high unemployment.

ADDITIONAL
RESOURCES

SELECTED BIBLIOGRAPHY

"Foster Care." *Children's Rights*, n.d., childrensrights.org.

"How to Help Children and Teens Manage Their Stress." *American Psychological Association*, 24 Oct. 2019, apa.org.

Mattera, Christina. "How to Talk to Your Parents after a Big Fight." *Girls' Life*, 19 Aug. 2019, girlslife.com.

FURTHER READINGS

Bialik, Mayim. *Girling Up: How to Be Strong, Smart, and Spectacular.* Philomel Books, 2017.

Myers, Carrie. *Coping with Stress and Pressure.* Abdo, 2021.

Solomon, Andrew. *Far from the Tree: How Children and Their Parents Learn to Accept One Another . . . Our Differences Unite Us.* Simon & Schuster Books for Young Readers, 2017.

ONLINE RESOURCES

Booklinks
NONFICTION NETWORK
FREE! ONLINE NONFICTION RESOURCES

To learn more about handling family challenges, please visit **abdobooklinks.com** or scan this QR code. These links are routinely monitored and updated to provide the most current information available.

MORE INFORMATION

For more information on this subject, contact or visit the following organizations:

Al-Anon Family Groups

1600 Corporate Landing Pkwy.
Virginia Beach, VA 23454-5617
al-anon.org
757-563-1600

Al-Anon provides support to people who have someone with an alcohol addiction in their lives. Its Alateen program focuses on supporting teenagers.

Feeding America

35 East Wacker Dr., Suite 2000
Chicago, IL 60601
feedingamerica.org
800-771-2303

Feeding America is a network of food banks that reaches nationwide. Its mission is to feed families and individuals across the United States.

Girls Inc.

120 Wall St.
New York, NY 10005
girlsinc.org
212-509-2000

This national organization focuses on long-term mentoring relationships and research-based programming to help girls grow up healthy, independent, and educated.

INDEX

ABOUT THE AUTHOR

REBECCA ROWELL

Rebecca Rowell has put her degree in publishing and writing to work as an editor and as an author, working on dozens of books in both roles. Recent topics as an author include the American middle class and the history of criminal law in the United States. Drafting this book made her reflect on her family and discover emotions she didn't realize she had. It was a good experience and will help her in the process of self-discovery. She lives in Minneapolis, Minnesota.